DISCOURSE SEVEN

IT'S ACHIEVABLE

BY

DR. YANNIQUE A. THOMAS

Copyright © 2020 by Yannique Thomas

All rights reserved. No part of this book may be reproduced in any form without written permission from the publisher.

Printed in the United States of America

Discourse Seven: It's Achievable

Revised Edition 2020

ISBN-13: 978-1-378-00778-3

ISBN-10: 1-378-00778-3

Lulu Press, Inc.

627 Davis Street

Suite 300

Morrisville, NC 27560

Table of Contents

THE AUTHOR

Yannique Angelique Helena nee (Whylly) Thomas was born in Nassau, Bahamas. She is the youngest of six siblings from Adrianna nee (McKinney) and Vivian Whylly Sr. She attended Yellow Elder Primary School in Nassau, Bahamas. She graduated high school from St. John's College in Nassau, Bahamas. She holds a Bachelor of Arts (BA) degree in International Studies from Barry University, a Master of Arts (MA) degree in International Relations from University of Oklahoma, and a Doctorate of Philosophy (PhD) in Organization and Management, Leadership specialization from Capella University. She is a graduate of the world-renowned leadership expert Dr. Myles Monroe (deceased) Leadership Seminar. She is a certified coach, teacher, speaker, trainer, and an executive director with The John Maxwell Team. She is proud to be a veteran, who has served as a military officer in the United States Army. She is a life member of the Military Officers Associations of America (MOAA), Reserve Officers Association (ROA), The American Legion, and a national legacy member of Zeta Phi Beta Sorority, Inc. She is the founder and President of Whay International, LLC, a leadership consulting group. She is the founder of It's Achievable Foundation, Inc. (IAFI) with a mission of eliminating adolescent and adult-illiteracy through providing reading and educational resources and programs, where to date over 1000 under privileged adolescent and adults have benefitted from reading supplies, book stipends, scholarships and literacy resources through the IAFI. She is a licensed minister and the founder of Legion of Deborah Ministries International (LODMI).

DEDICATION

To my extraordinary mother, Adrianna, Albertha nee (McKinney) Whylly. I could never have become anything without your example. You are my hero and everything that I could ever hope to become. It would not be possible for me to be the woman that God made me to be today without your love, support and daily encouragement to embrace my uniqueness and to keep moving forward. Thank you for always reminding me that the sky is the limit, that I could accomplish anything that I set my mind to become and that I could achieve anything that I wanted to achieve as long as I am willing to work until I achieve it.

To my siblings…Denise (deceased), Michaela, Linda (deceased), Vivian, Jr., and Paul (deceased), thank you for leading the way for me and for always encouraging me to be fearless and to dream the unthinkable and to do the impossible.

To all of my family and friends, thank you for your unyielding love and support.

PREFACE

I wrote this book to inspire someone to dare to dream and to have the courage to pursue their passion. We know that all things are possible with God and that everything is ACHIEVABLE as long as you stay the course. The confidence that I felt in taking back my power by overcoming the feelings of failure and rejection has emboldened my faith in sharing with each person that I meet that no matter what anyone says to you or about you, anything that you want and willing to pursue with all of your heart, mind, body and soul is ACHIEVABLE. For instance, I believe that I was put on the earth to teach, liberate and to set the captive free by eliminating illiteracy through providing reading resources and programs. I feel compelled to inspire the world to READ in order to lead in every area of your life. I truly believe that the power to achieve is in your ability to READ. This way you are able to research things on your own so that when rejection comes opportunity is given birth to re-present your God given idea in a completely different way so that your dream does not die inside of you but it is actualized into to reality.

INTRODUCTION

"IT'S ACHIEVABLE"

It's ACHIEVABLE…anything that you set your mind to. It's ACHIEVABLE …if you are willing to give it all that you have. It's ACHIEVABLE …if you are willing to give up everything that you have. It's ACHIEVABLE …if you can see it, you can have it. It's ACHIEVABLE …anything that you put your mind to. It's ACHIEVABLE …the key is to keep on moving forward. It's ACHIEVABLE …you are not someone else's opinion. It's ACHIEVABLE …because you are perfect in everyway. It's ACHIEVABLE …to uncover you buried dreams. It's ACHIEVABLE …because time is on your side. It's ACHIEVABLE …the sky is the limit…It's ACHIEVABLE ….and so it is…SELAH and AMEN!

Chapter One

In the Beginning – My Extended Family

The "It's Achievable" journey began for me on January 11, 1971 when I was born Yannique Angelique Helena Whylly to Vivian and Adrianna nee (McKinney) Whylly. I am the youngest of six siblings of my parents. I have two brothers Vivian Jr. and Paul (deceased) from my mother and two more brothers Vincent and Dave from my father. I have three sisters Denise (deceased), Michaela and Linda (deceased) from my mother and one additional sister Jackie from my father. I have three nephews Vincent Jr., Gary Jr. and Karis and six nieces Samantha, Raquel, Chantal, Gareece, Robyn and Allison.

I grew up in a somewhat middle income subdivision called Yellow Elder. This residential community was very close knit for the most part but was known for its regular trouble makers and offenders that frequented the main police station on the main road called Baillou Hill Road. Our house was a modest three bedroom one bathroom home facing the main road, in which my parents added a room that was a den filled with books of all sorts, Britannica encyclopedias, comic books, Nancy Drew, See Jane Run books and Mills & Boons for my eldest sister that was in college to name a few. I attended Yellow Elder Primary, which was the public elementary school in the neighborhood that I grew up in. I was friends with all the children of the neighborhood. My family was well known among the families in the neighborhood. Some of my neighborhood friends that I can remember were Deborah Charlton, Natasha Symonnette, Samantha Cartwright, Ann King, and Charlene Murphy. Some of the neighborhood families that I can recall were the Symonnette's, Cartwright's, Charlton's, Brennan's, Burrow's, King's, Bowe's, Turnquest's, Stockdale's, Johnson's, Godfrey's, Stirrup's, Brown's, McKenzie's, Murphy's, Bodie's, Cash's and a host of other families.

From the time that I was four years old, I was allowed to go to school. I officially entered the first grade at the age of four. I always remember enjoying primary school. I am not sure why, but it was some place that I actually looked forward to going to everyday. I was told by my teachers that I was a good student and that I loved to read. I was very popular and had great teachers. I can remember the names of my elementary school teachers. My first-grade teacher was Mrs. Charlton. She was the most impressionable teacher on my young life. I remember having the fondest love for her exclusively, as if she was my mother. She paid me one of the greatest compliments of naming one of her daughters "Yannique" after me. My second-grade teacher was Ms. Brown. I recall her being very strict. My third-grade teacher was Mrs. Rollins. She was a charm and always had a very special place in my heart. She picked up where Mrs. Charlton left off in the first grade. She was warm, loving, and firm, but fair and a great teacher. She possessed a heart for learning just like Ms. Charlton did. She would give me rides home from school from time to time after my family moved to Cable Beach where she lived. I also had Ms. Holland. She was a Caucasian teacher from Europe. She had to be very open minded especially to be teaching in the Bahamas in the seventies immersed in an all-Black school as the only Caucasian person. My fourth grade teachers were Mrs. Saunders and Ms. Roker. The fourth grade was called center four. Ms. Roker was my main teacher. She was the first person to introduce me to learning bible verses. I remember learning to recite Psalm 23 in center four with Ms. Roker. She was about four feet tall, a ball of fire for God, an exceptional communicator and a great teacher.

My fifth grade teacher was Mr. Sweeting. He was a musician and a teacher. Mr. Sweeting was tall, slanky and a good disciplinarian.

My six grade teachers were Ms. Bain and Mrs. Cumberbatch. I was very fond of both of them. They were both exceptional teachers. All of Mrs. Cumberbatch's children attended the school, Lynette, Charmaine and Kenneth. I was good friends with Charmaine because we were in the same year group and had classes together. She is still one of the most kind and sweetest persons that I have ever met to date. We all ended up attending private high school together at St. John's College.

Mrs. Ford was my principal from grades one through four. She was an icon. Everyone in the community knew Ms. Ford for her standard elegant hairstyle, speech and appearance. Mrs. Collie was my principal until I graduated primary school. She was a modest, cordial and polite lady. I am extremely grateful to God for such humble beginnings. I am even blessed all the more for having such a happy childhood.

Chapter Two

My High School Years

When I was in the sixth grade my family moved to a neighborhood that was far away from the primary school and all of the family and friends that I grew up with. This was a very difficult and traumatic time in my life. My mother decided to move out from the family home with me and my siblings for our safety. My father was the disciplinary in my family. He was very strict and never wanted any of us to hang out over at our friend's houses or outside on the streets. He always made us read books. It was a non-negotiable. This early childhood experience fueled my passion for learning, reading and teaching. Instead of going outside, I learned how to entertain myself. On a daily basis, I would pretend to be a reading teacher with all the Muppet show characters as my students. I would faithfully teach them how to read and write and correct them with a spanking from a 12 inch ruler if they were unruly and would not pay attention. My parents never officially divorced but decided to live separately until my father's death in 2008.

When I was in the fifth grade, my mother started our first business in the den of our home. We had enough books to start a used book store trade program. All of the neighborhood kids could bring any book and trade it for twenty-five cents. The books ranged from comic books to Nancy Drew to See Jane Run books and Mills and Boons. By the time that I was in the sixth grade, this home book business had expanded into an official business in its own building known as 'Denise's Bookerteria". Denise Bookerteria had expanded to selling more than used books. The store had expanded to selling toys, snacks, clothing, new books, school supplies and other stationary items.

After graduating elementary school, I attended St. John's College. It was not a college as in the traditional idea of post-secondary education, but it was the same as a high school. It was the name given to it because it was a private religious school. It was very similar to a private catholic school but instead was an Anglican (Episcopalian) school. It was there that I began to experience doubt in my ability to achieve academic success. Even though I was a great student in elementary school, my high school experience was challenging. I was not reading as much in high school as I did when I was in elementary school and it showed in my academic performance.

I knew that I was intelligent but at that time I lacked the personal discipline of reading which was required to continue to excel in high school. I was also battling with a situation where I was in a one parent household and the daughter of an entrepreneur. My mother was the only bread winner for the family so I had to help my mother out with the family business during the week days after school and all day on the weekends. This was a major distractor for me in applying myself more academically.

Upon graduating high school, I wanted to attend college. I had always dreamed of studying International Relations from the time that I was in the 8th grade. When I was in the 8th grade, my mother took me on a three week vacation to Asia. We visited Hong Kong, Bangkok in Thailand, Manila in the Philippines and Singapore. This experience impacted my life forever. Since I had visited all those countries, I was inspired to read up about other countries like Germany, London, France and Italy and had visited them through the imagination of books until I was able to physically visit them. I was fully persuaded at that young age that knowledge was power and that being literate was important. I realized that literacy through reading would allow me to go places through the power of my imagination without having to physical go there. This to me was both empowering and fascinating.

I was convinced that I would never be able attend college no matter how much I wanted to because I knew that I had never done well on multiple choice exams in the past. I did eventually take the SAT (Scholastic Aptitude Test) and as expected the results were low. This was very humbly for me to accept. I was very devastated. I could not understand this because I knew that I was intelligent. Despite how other people made me feel, I never ever accepted that this made me dumb, stupid or ignorant. I made a decision at that stage in my life that I would read to find out every alternative method to accomplishing my academic goals. I read and researched colleges that offered tutoring and extra classes for the subject areas that I needed help with. The bottom line is because I could read I never accepted no for an answer. As long as you can read, you will achieve. I wrote this short book to inspire at least one person or student to dear to dream and pursue their passion because it is achievable as long as you are able to READ.

Chapter Three

My College Years

When I graduated high school, my mother was not very eager for me to attend college because she wanted me to stay and manage the family business. However, I wanted to attend college. I did not tell my mother about my low SAT scores. I applied to colleges anyway knowing that I probably would not get accepted. I eventually got accepted conditionally into Barry University in Miami, Florida. I had to do a lot of extra classes and extra credit work to gain full acceptance. This transition was very difficult for me. I spent the next seven years working to complete my Bachelor of Arts degree in International Studies. I faced many obstacles. For example, I experienced a mental overload during one semester of college from the pressure of being the primary care giver for my oldest sister who had stage-four cancer. A few years earlier, I watched my mother care for one of her younger sisters, my aunt until she died from breast cancer. I was so overwhelmed with her illness at such a young age; I could not focus to sit my final exams. The thought of losing my sister at such a young age to the same breast cancer was extremely devastating to me. The result of this was a grade of 'F' for each of the five classes that I took that term that counted against my grade point average (GPA). I was so devastated by this that I wanted to completely give up on my dream of getting my degree and drop out of college and just move on with my life because I knew that I was smarter than those “F” grades that I had received. I took the next year and a half to two years off from college before returning to complete my degree. I spent that time healing from the diagnosis of my sister, while working in various jobs trying to figure out what is it that I was put on the earth to do. However, it took every fiber in me but I eventually returned to college and on 9 May 1997, I officially graduated with a Bachelor of Arts in International Studies from Barry University. My sister eventually made it through her initial surgeries, chemotherapy and was able to attend my graduation, but she lost her battle to cancer in 1999.

Achieving my Bachelor of Arts was such an accomplishment that I could not just stop there. Ever since the day that I felt the shame of my low SAT scores, I dreamed of achieving my doctorate degree. I was not sure in what but I knew that I wanted to achieve it. I developed a deep passion to inspire other people or students that did not show traditional academic promise that they could achieve anything that they set their mind to in spite of what anyone or anything outside of them predicted, if they learned how to READ.

While I was living in Mannheim, Germany I applied to the University of Oklahoma to get a Master of Arts degree in International Relations. I was accepted in March 2003 and graduated in December 2005 with my Master of Arts degree in International Relations. There were many challenges with achieving this degree. I had my final work rejected over and over again but I stayed the course made all of the necessary corrections until I submitted the work that met the standard for degree completion. Each time my work was rejected, I felt a part of me just wanting to throw in the towel and give up but through perseverance and determination I stayed the course and received the award of completing my degree. However, I could not stop there because of all the challenges that I overcame. I had to keep on going until I achieved my doctorate degree. In July 2007 I applied and was accepted to Capella University School of Business and Technology to complete a Doctorate of Philosophy in Organization and Management, Leadership. The ability to achieve these goals reinforced for me that anything that you put your mind to is achievable, as long as you are willing and able to READ.

Chapter Four

Present – From Then to Now

In 2008 I took a leave of absence from my doctoral program to enlist in the United States Army to attend Officer Candidate School (OCS) at Fort Benning, Georgia. I was 36 years old when I attended and graduated basic training, where the average age of enlistment was 17-18 years old. I graduated from OCS in August 2010, and was commissioned as a second lieutenant later that year.

Upon commissioning I was assigned to my first duty station as a Second Lieutenant as the Battalion S1 Officer in Charge of Personnel Management and as the Adjutant for the 317th Military Police Battalion located in Tampa, Florida from 2008-2012. I was selected as the first African American female officer to hold the position of Company Commander of the Headquarter Headquarter Detachment (HHD), 317th Military Police Battalion and in my battalion's, history located in Tampa, Florida from 2012-2014. I was ordered to active duty as a protocol officer at United States Central Command (USCENTCOM) located at MacDill Air force Base, Tampa, Florida from 2014-2015. During this assignment, I was selected as one of the protocol officers to officially escort the 44th President of the United States, President Barack Obama on his official visit.

My military awards and decorations include the Army Meritorious Service Medal, Army Commendation Medal, Joint Service Commendation Medal, National Defense Service Medal, Global War on Terrorism Service Medal, Army Service Ribbon, and the Armed Forces Reserve Medal.

Currently, I am the founder of the It's Achievable Foundation, Inc., where I serve as the Chief Executive Officer. I am the founder and President of WHAY International LLC, where we provide consulting services in leadership, management, coaching, training, education, career, strategy and advising for groups or individuals. I am also an executive director with The John Maxwell Team, where I am certified to coach, teach, train, and speak.

The reason that I am sharing my story is not to brag, but to inspire at least one person that may be struggling in their life professionally, educationally, or in any other area of your life. I am sharing this to inspire you to know that you have the ability within you to choose what your destiny will be despite any obvious facts, obstacles or limiting beliefs that anyone else may have of you or what you may hold of yourself. God and life in general is no respecter of persons. I am someone that was a terrible test taker that scored less than a 600 on my scholastic Aptitude Test (SAT). This was a clear indicator that I was not supposed to graduate college or amount to anything much. Not to mention that I barely graduated with my bachelor's degree, because I was one of the primary caregivers for my oldest sister, who was being treated for stage four cancer during that time. But some-how I went on to achieve my Master of Arts degree with much resilience, and then to achieving my first PhD degree with great determination, of which I graduated with honors.

Achieving my first PhD and graduating the military officer candidate school were among the top two most challenging accomplishments that I have achieved to date. The only goal greater is my passion and desire to eliminate global illiteracy through providing reading resources and programs throughout the world. However, I must confess that it was not easy. But all things came together for my good because of what I set my mind to do, what I was willing to give up, and I was determined to believe only what I say about myself. I am here as a testament for everyone reading this to know that if God can do it for me, he will surely do it for you. The only thing that you must do is be determined and willing to put in the work. Because hard work must pay off.

Chapter Five

Conclusion

It is worth noting that all of those accolades are meaningless, if I am not able to impact one person or student to dare to dream and become a READER. True success to some people could be having a lot of degrees and money. True success for me is to be able to get up every day and pursue my passion like I am doing today. My passion, my dream, and my goal is to inspire at least one person or student to become a reader in order to ACHIEVE, LEAD, BE WEALTHY and ADVANCE.

Overcoming the feelings of failure and rejection from my low SAT scores has emboldened my faith in sharing with each person or student that I meet that no matter what the facts may be that is not your truth. No matter what anyone says to you or about you that does not line up with what you want for yourself, please disregard and ignore it because anything that you want is achievable if you believe that you can achieve it and can READ to find out the necessary information to assist you in achieving your goal.

I feel compelled to inspire the world to READ in order to lead in every area of life. I truly believe that the power to achieve is in your ability to READ and research things on your own so that when rejection comes opportunity is given birth to through relentless research and your ability to READ. I hope that this story encourages at least one person or student to always remember that anything is ACHIEVABLE once you put your mind to it and you are able to READ. Always remember that IT'S ACHIEVABLE, all you have to do is believe first that you can achieve your goal.

Chapter Six

It's Achievable Foundation, Inc.

In an effort to eliminate global illiteracy among adolescents and adults, especially in low-income and underprivileged communities, I was inspired to start the It's Achievable Foundation, Inc. The foundation is organized to increase public awareness of juvenile and adult illiteracy and to focus public awareness on solutions to stopping and preventing illiteracy. A primary purpose of the foundation is to provide reading resources, book stipends, scholarships, literacy events, and educational programs to help as many people as possible to learn how to read or to become a reader.

If you are interested in finding out more information about the foundation and our programs or about volunteering with our organization, you may do so by emailing: itsachievablefoundation@gmail.com.

If you're interested in making a tax-deductible contribution to the foundation, you may do so by sending a check or money order to: It's Achievable Foundation, Inc., P.O. Box 48372, Tampa, FL 33646.

THANK YOU FOR YOUR SUPPORT!

Personal Notes

Personal Notes

Personal Notes

Personal Notes

Personal Notes

Personal Notes

www.ingramcontent.com/pod-product-compliance
Ingram Content Group UK Ltd.
Pitfield, Milton Keynes, MK11 3LW, UK
UKHW020137250726
13967UKWH00002B/704

9 781387 007783